WHEN THE CLOUDS CAME

Story & Photos
by
Kimberly Williamson

illustrations by
Frank Fernandez

All rights reserved. No part of this book may be reproduced or used in any manner without the prior written permission of the copyright owner, except for the use of brief quotations in a book review.
Copyright @ 2020 by Kimberly Williamson
ISBN: 978-0-578-77149-6
Library of Congress Control Number: 2020918442
First Edition
Peak Blaze Press
Peakblazepress.com

I dedicate this story of hope to every cloudy moment faced during the year 2020. We are the light.

I dedicate this book of photographs to Jarod, Tobin & Natalie. During the pandemic, we left no stone unturned finding our happiness through adventures in the wilderness of North Carolina.

-Kimberly Williamson

To Kimberly, for entrusting me with her special 'gem' of a story, I am grateful.

To my wife, Lisa, and our two sons, Alex & Jason. Thank you for always being supportive of every creative endeavor I pursue.

To our reader, never stop reading, learning, or imagining.

-Frank Fernandez

CHARACTERS :

ROSE

CLOVER

SPECKLES

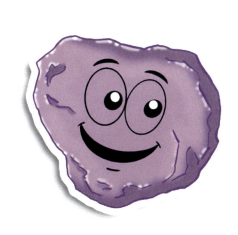

PETAL

"They look like connect the dots!" shouted **ROSE**.

"They look like fireflies!" shrieked **CLOVER**.

"They look like nightlights!" yelled **SPECKLES**.

"They look like millions of campfires!" exclaimed **PETAL**.

EACH DAY THE FOUR STONES FOCUSED ON FINDING THE PERFECT SPOT FOR STARING AT THE LUMINOUS SKY.

They couldn't wait for nightfall to soak in the brightness of the stars.

Sometimes the clear blue skies made the daytime seem just too long for them to bear.

ROSE, CLOVER, SPECKLES, and **PETAL** blazed trails through the forest while the sun's rays shone upon the peaks and fields before them.

They debated between the low ground and high ground to settle and wait for their evening routine.

They discussed grassy patches and shallow streams. All their energy focused on finding the best place to view the beauty of the starlit sky.

THERE WAS NEVER A FEAR OF NOT BEING ABLE TO SEE THE STARS;

it was always just
a question of the best
place to view them.

However,
nature is ever-changing;
nothing is **promised.**

THE STONES decided to stargaze from atop a small waterfall. There was a cool breeze misting off the flowing water. Everything was as expected.

The sun had begun to set as they lay next to one another, eyes targeted on the endless sky above.

They watched **the sun** disappear.

They waited for **the stars** to shine.

BUT THE SKY JUST TURNED STARK BLACK.

They could not see
one another.

They could not see
any stars.

They could only hear
the waterfall.

AT FIRST, THE STONES PANICKED.

There were no magical stars.
There was no reliable starlight.
There was no light at all.

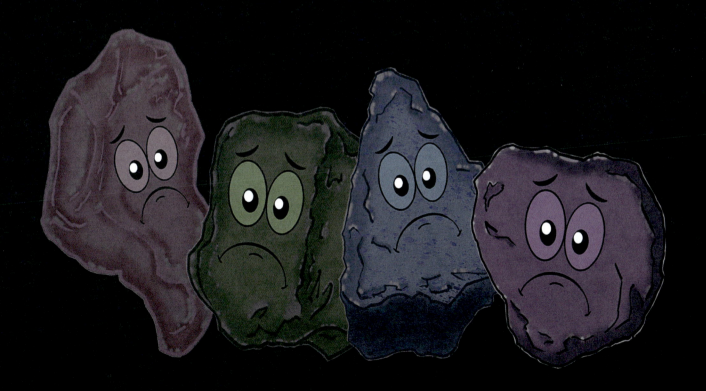

CLOVER, who loved the fireflies, worried he would never see them again.

ROSE, who loved to connect the dots, missed playing.

PETAL, who loved the campfires, pouted that she didn't know how to feel warm without them.

SPECKLES, who loved the nightlights, cried that he was afraid of the dark.

EACH STONE WAS SILENT, FIXATED ON THE UNKNOWN, AND UPSET ABOUT AN UNEXPECTED LOSS.

Then, Clover saw a blink.
It was a real-life firefly.
Clover called out to the others!

THEIR EYES WIDENED AS THEY AWOKE FROM THEIR FEAR AND NOTICED THE BLINKING CREATURES.

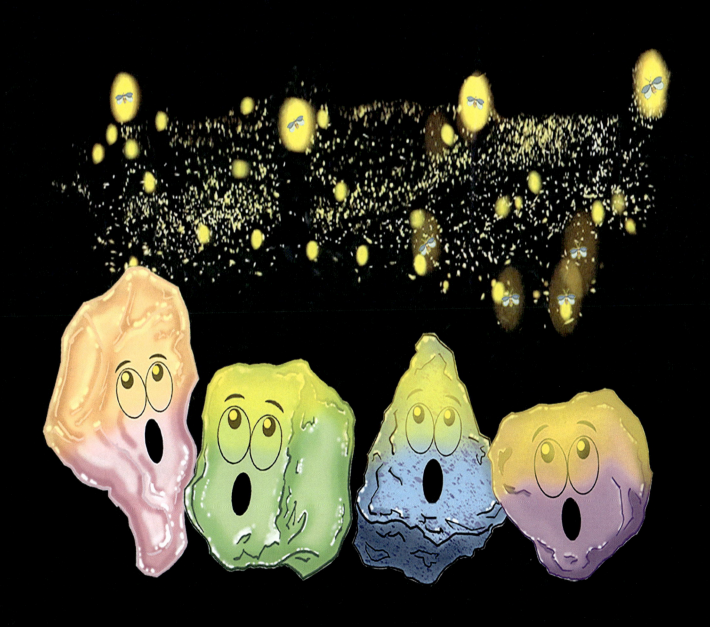

THE STONES STARED IN AWE AT THE FIREFLIES' WINGS AND RADIANT BODIES.

They followed the gleaming trails left by the fireflies dancing around them.

The stones cheered in excitement over each one they spotted.

THE DARKNESS FADED AS NIGHT TURNED INTO DAY, AND SLIVERS OF LIGHT PEEKED THROUGH THE CLOUDS THAT CONTINUED TO LOOM.

The stones looked up; all they had known transformed so quickly. Then Rose noticed shapes in the clouds.

The sky was always so clear during the day, which made for beautiful viewing at night. But the clouds, surprisingly, brought new sights, like a giant penguin.

PETAL FELT WARM FROM FRIENDSHIP. ROSE FOUND NEW WAYS TO PLAY. CLOVER CHASED FIREFLIES. SPECKLES LEARNED TO SHINE.

Petal, Rose, Clover, and Speckles began to feel safe realizing that they each had cloudy challenges, but they were all finding hope. The four friends were more than stones sitting still as the world moved; they were gemstones shining in the darkness.

THEN SHE SAW AN ELEPHANT, A BUNNY, A ROOSTER, AND A RACE CAR!

Rose never saw these figures before in the sky. Each one she discovered made her want to search for more.

PETAL NOTICED THAT SPECKLES SPARKLED AS HE SMILED AT HER.

Speckles explained that he was smiling because **Petal's** shade of purple matched the **beautiful wildflowers** growing around them.

This compliment made **Petal** feel warm inside, just like the thought of campfires. **Speckles** realized he was creating light, under the covered sky, by sharing **kindness.**

AS THE DAY CONTINUED,

they still explored the low ground and high ground, grassy patches, and shallow streams. All the places they considered as a clearing to view the stars when everything was still the same.

However, today they were not focused on the landscape as a place to wait. This time, Speckles, Clover, Petal, and Rose noticed small leaves of different shapes, colors, and textures. Some leaves hung from tall trees, while others extended from low plants. The leaves were still growing and so were the stones.

THE HUNT FOR THE NEXT UNIQUE LEAF BROUGHT LAUGHTER AMONG THE FRIENDS.

As they reached a stream, the rushing water made the stones stop immediately. The sound reminded them of the small waterfall and the moment that everything changed.

Life today was different from lying in the grass and looking up at the bright stars. They wondered who else was striving to understand the world beneath the clouds.

WITH THAT THOUGHT, THEY COLLECTED THEIR FAVORITE LEAVES.

The stones gently placed the leaves in the water and smiled.

Rose, Clover, Speckles, and Petal floated the leaves downstream to share a sunny feeling with others amidst the haze. They certainly missed the beauty of the night sky, but they found beauty in other places too.

THE CLOUDS WOULD EVENTUALLY LEAVE BECAUSE NOTHING STAYS THE SAME FOREVER.

But the stones would never forget what they saw, felt, and **LEARNED** when the clouds came.

FOLLOW PEAK BLAZE PRESS TO SEE WHERE ROSE, CLOVER, SPECKLES, AND PETAL ARE NOW!

 @PeakBlazePress

 @peakblazepress

Made in the USA
Columbia, SC
09 December 2020